SEPARATION OF POWERS

THE IMPORTANCE OF CHECKS AND BALANCES

JACK READER

NEW YORK

Published in 2018 by The Rosen Publishing Group, Inc.
29 East 21st Street, New York, NY 10010

Editor: Melissa Raé Shofner
Book Design: Michael Flynn
Interior Layout: Reann Nye

Photo Credits: Cover (Capitol building) Brandon Bourdages/Shutterstock.com; cover, p. 15 (White House) turtix/Shutterstock.com; cover, p. 15 (Supreme Court building) Steven Frame/Shutterstock.com; p. 5 Blend Images - Hill Street Studios/Brand X Pictures/Getty Images; p. 7 https://en.wikipedia.org/wiki/File:Flickr_-_USCapitol_-_The_First_Continental_Congress,_1774.jpg; p. 8 https://commons.wikimedia.org/wiki/File:JohnLocke.png; p. 9 https://commons.wikimedia.org/wiki/File:Locke_treatises_of_government_page.jpg; pp. 9, 15 (background) Evgeny Karandaev/Shutterstock.com; p. 10 Everett Historical/Shutterstock.com; p. 11 https://commons.wikimedia.org/wiki/File:Montesquieu,_De_l%27Esprit_des_loix_(1st_ed,_1748,_vol_1,_title_page).jpg; p. 12 https://commons.wikimedia.org/wiki/File:James_Madison.jpg; p.13 https://en.wikipedia.org/wiki/Signing_of_the_United_States_Constitution#/media/File:Scene_at_the_Signing_of_the_Constitution_of_the_United_States.jpg; p. 15 (Capitol building) Diego Grandi/Shutterstock.com; p. 17 https://commons.wikimedia.org/wiki/File:Gilbert_Stuart_Williamstown_Portrait_of_George_Washington.jpg; p. 18 https://en.wikipedia.org/wiki/Dwight_D._Eisenhower#/media/File:Dwight_D._Eisenhower,_official_Presidential_portrait.jpg; pp. 19, 25 Bettmann/Getty Images; p. 20 Pool/Getty Images News/Getty Images; p. 21 Chip Somodevilla/Getty Images News/Getty Images; pp. 22–23 PAUL J. RICHARDS/AFP/Getty Images; p. 27 Stock Montage/Archive Photos/Getty Images; p. 29 https://commons.wikimedia.org/wiki/File:Prise_de_la_Bastille.jpg.

Cataloging-in-Publication Data

Names: Reader, Jack.
Title: Separation of powers: the importance of checks and balances / Jack Reader.
Description: New York : PowerKids Press, 2018. | Series: Spotlight on civic action | Includes index.
Identifiers: ISBN 9781538327937 (pbk.) | ISBN 9781508163992 (library bound) | ISBN 9781538328057 (6 pack)
Subjects: LCSH: Separation of powers--United States--Juvenile literature. | United States--Politics and government--Juvenile literature.
Classification: LCC JK305.R43 2018 | DDC 320.473'04--dc23

Manufactured in China

CPSIA Compliance Information: Batch #BW18PK For further information contact Rosen Publishing, New York, New York at 1-800-237-9932.

CONTENTS

CHAPTER ONE

DIVIDING POWER

You might know that the U.S. federal government is divided into three branches. These include the executive branch (president, vice president, and cabinet), legislative branch (U.S. Congress), and the judicial branch (U.S. court system). But do you know why? The federal government's three branches were designed to help create a separation of powers between key governmental positions. This separation of powers protects American citizens from political **corruption** and **tyrants**.

Why is a separation of powers between the branches important? Imagine if the president made laws instead of Congress. And imagine if the president also ran the courts. A president with that much power would be very close to a monarch, or king, which is something the Founding Fathers wanted to avoid when establishing the United States of America.

Can you imagine what it would be like if the United States was ruled by a king or emperor instead of three balanced branches? Life would likely be very different than it is today.

CHAPTER TWO

COLONIAL ROOTS

By looking at U.S. colonial history, we can see why a separation of powers is so important to the United States and its citizens. During the late colonial period, King George III and Parliament, the British lawmaking body, decided to tax the colonies to help pay for wars fought on colonial soil. Some colonists, called Loyalists, wanted to remain faithful to the British. Others were unhappy. They felt the colonies were being unfairly taxed, especially because they weren't allowed to have representatives in British Parliament.

It was clear to the Founding Fathers that, in order to avoid creating another monarchy, they needed a strongly **democratic** constitution. They created a government that had three branches, as well as a system of checks and balances to help keep those branches from becoming too powerful or corrupt.

The First Continental Congress met in 1774 to create a list of complaints for King George III. After the list was ignored, the Second Continental Congress met in 1775 to create the Declaration of Independence and break free of British rule.

CHAPTER THREE

GREAT POLITICAL THINKERS

The first people to write about the idea of a government with multiple branches were the ancient Greeks. The philosopher Aristotle (384–322 BC) theorized about a three-part government made up of monarchy, **aristocracy**, and democracy.

Plymouth Colony in Massachusetts, established in 1620, had one of the first European governments in North America. The colonists established a biparty government, meaning it had two branches. The General Court served as a judicial and legislative branch. The executive branch was made up of a governor and seven assistants.

In *Two Treatises of Government* (1689), English political philosopher John Locke examined the monarchy in England at the time. Locke supported a biparty system consisting of the monarchy (executive branch) and a lawmaking body (legislative branch). Locke's ideas inspired young governments worldwide.

JOHN LOCKE

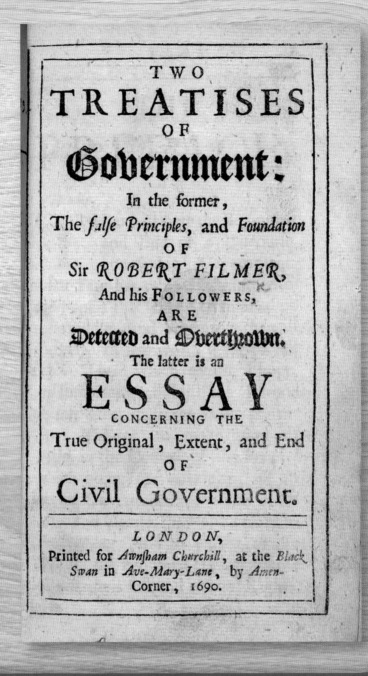

TWO
TREATISES
OF
Government:
In the former,
The false Principles, and Foundation
OF
Sir ROBERT FILMER,
And his FOLLOWERS,
ARE
Detected and Overthrown.
The latter is an
ESSAY
CONCERNING THE
True Original, Extent, and End
OF
Civil Government.

LONDON,
Printed for Awnsham Churchill, at the Black
Swan in Ave-Mary-Lane, by Amen-
Corner, 1690.

In *Two Treatises of Government,* Locke stated that all men are equal under God and that any rightful government needs the consent of the people it rules. Otherwise, the people have the right to overthrow the government.

Montesquieu was a French political philosopher. In his 1748 book *The Spirit of the Laws*, he looked at contemporary English politics to explain his revolutionary political ideas. He wrote that the "state" that truly wanted to promote liberty needed three branches of government. Montesquieu's words, shown here, explain how a single ruler can lead to problems.

Montesquieu spent much of his life reading philosophic works about politics. His theory of the separation of powers influenced the Founding Fathers to create three branches of the federal government.

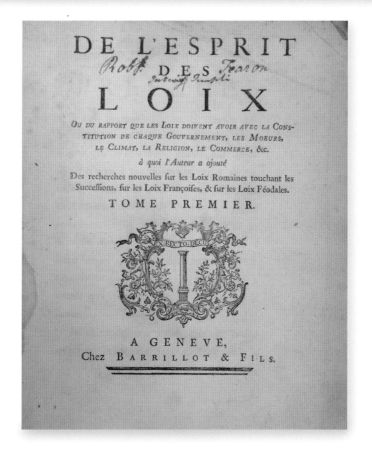

Were [the judicial branch] joined with the legislative, the life and liberty of the subject would be exposed to **arbitrary** control; for the judge would then be the legislator. Were it joined to the executive power, the judge might behave with violence and **oppression**. There would be an end of everything, were the same man, or the same body, whether of the nobles or of the people, to exercise those three powers, that of enacting laws, that of executing the public resolutions, and of trying the causes of individuals.

—Charles-Louis de Secondat, baron de La Brède et de Montesquieu, *De l'esprit des loix (The Spirit of the Laws)*

THE U.S. CONSTITUTION

The Founding Fathers didn't write the U.S. Constitution overnight. It took many months for them to agree to its final version. It also took the influence of such thinkers as Aristotle, Locke, Montesquieu, and others. Studying the works of these great political thinkers helped spark democracy in the colonies. The Founding Fathers wanted to create a government that could be held accountable for its actions.

James Madison, a representative from Virginia, played a major role in crafting the separation of powers section of the Constitution. The result

JAMES MADISON

Some critics of the U.S. Constitution felt there wasn't enough separation between the three branches of government. Madison argued it wasn't practical—or the intent of Montesquieu—to have a complete separation of powers.

was the "Madisonian Model," which features a separation of powers with a system of checks and balances. Madison and his followers believed the Constitution granted power to the branches but also kept them from becoming too powerful on their own.

CHAPTER FIVE

BREAKING DOWN THE BRANCHES

The executive branch is made up of the president and his cabinet. This branch is in charge of executing, or carrying out, the country's laws.

Congress, or the legislative branch, makes laws. It is a bicameral branch, which means it's made up of two legislative bodies: the Senate and the House of Representatives. The politicians in Congress are elected by the people. The Senate has 100 members, two from each state. The House has 435 representatives. Larger states have more representatives in the House.

The judicial branch is made up of the Supreme Court and many lesser courts. Supreme Court justices are appointed by the president and serve for life.

These three branches work closely with each other for the good of the people. Let's look at how each branch checks the other branches to ensure true democracy.

LEGISLATIVE BRANCH

- MAKES LAWS
- APPROVES PRESIDENTAL APPOINTMENTS
- TWO SENATORS FROM EACH STATE
- THE NUMBER OF CONGRESSMEN IS BASED ON POPULATION

JUDICIAL BRANCH

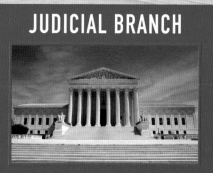

- DECIDES IF LAWS ARE CONSTITUTIONAL
- NINE JUSTICES
- JUSTICES APPOINTED BY THE PRESIDENT
- CAN OVERTURN RULINGS BY OTHER JUDGES

EXECUTIVE BRANCH

- SIGNS LAWS
- VETOES LAWS
- PARDONS PEOPLE
- APPOINTS FEDERAL JUDGES
- ELECTED EVERY FOUR YEARS

Each branch of the U.S. government has special powers. Each branch also has important checks on the other branches.

CHAPTER SIX

EXECUTIVE BRANCH

There are several key ways the executive branch keeps the legislative branch in check. Perhaps the most well-known power is the veto. Veto power allows the president to reject bills that have been approved by Congress. This stops them from becoming laws. The president has 10 days to review a bill that passes both houses of Congress. He can accept the bill and allow it to become a law, or he can veto it. However, Congress can overrule the veto with a two-thirds vote. This is another example of one branch checking the other.

The executive branch can call on Congress when it's not in session. This last happened in 1948 when President Harry S. Truman called on both houses to meet in an attempt to force them to pass legislation on several important issues.

The first presidential veto occurred in 1792. George Washington vetoed a bill that would have raised the number of northern representatives in the House of Representatives. Washington rejected the bill because it would have gone against the Constitution and was unfair for southern states.

The executive branch also has ways to limit the power of the judicial branch. The president appoints judges to the Supreme Court. Often, Republican presidents nominate **conservative** justices, and Democratic presidents nominate **liberal** justices. Justices

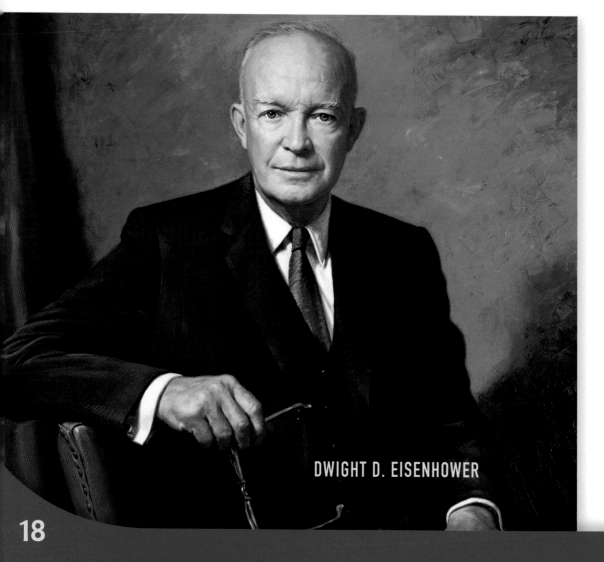

DWIGHT D. EISENHOWER

Presidents can sign executive orders that are much like federal laws. These orders are subject to review by the other branches. In 1957, President Dwight Eisenhower issued an executive order and put the Arkansas National Guard under federal control. He did this to enforce **desegregation** in Little Rock schools.

serve for life, so an appointment to the Supreme Court often means many years of support for the president's political party. The decisions of Supreme Court justices are often influential and long lasting, which is another benefit for the president's party, even after he leaves office.

It's not clearly mentioned in the U.S. Constitution, but in some cases, the president can resist judicial efforts to **subpoena** the executive branch for information. This is called executive privilege. The president can also pardon people who've been found guilty in a court of law.

CHAPTER SEVEN

LEGISLATIVE BRANCH

The executive branch isn't the only one that can limit the power of the other branches. The president nominates Supreme Court justices, but Congress needs to approve them first. The Senate Judiciary Committee reviews the president's nominees, then the Senate votes on them. The Senate can reject the president's nominees with a majority vote (at least 51 out of 100).

Congress can also vote to remove a president (or another executive official) from office for committing a

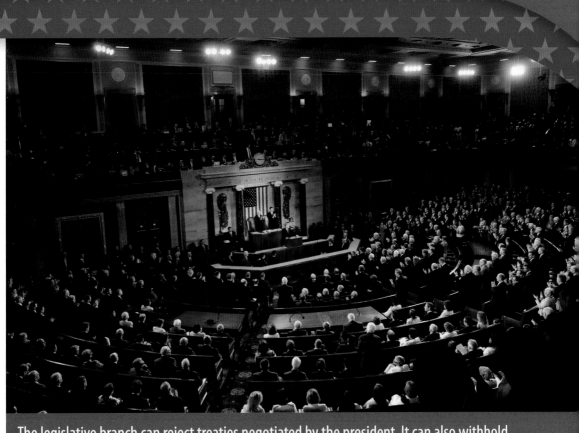

The legislative branch can reject treaties negotiated by the president. It can also withhold funding from presidential plans and programs.

crime. The beginning of this process is called impeachment. The House of Representatives begins a president's impeachment by introducing a bill or passing a resolution. If the bill or resolution passes by a majority vote, the president then stands trial before the Senate with the chief justice of the Supreme Court as the judge. A two-thirds vote in the Senate is needed to make a **conviction**.

Congress can also impeach Supreme Court justices. In fact, this is the only way for the government to punish and remove a justice from the Supreme Court. The House of Representatives needs a majority vote to start the impeachment process. If the vote succeeds, the case is sent to the Senate for a trial. Again, a two-thirds vote in the Senate is needed to make a conviction. Only one justice has gone through this process. In 1805, Justice Samuel

Chase was impeached for improper conduct. However, he wasn't found guilty and remained on the court until his death in 1811.

Perhaps the most powerful check Congress can place on the judicial branch is to create amendments to overcome judicial decisions. However, in the end, the Supreme Court has the power to declare an amendment unconstitutional.

In December 1998, members of the House Judiciary Committee discussed articles of impeachment against President Bill Clinton. However, President Clinton wasn't found guilty.

CHAPTER EIGHT

JUDICIAL BRANCH

The powers given to the judicial branch by the Constitution are designed to keep the executive and legislative branches from becoming too strong. The judicial branch is often thought of as the weakest branch. It cannot make or enforce laws. However, the Supreme Court has a power called judicial interpretation. This means it has the power to determine what executive and legislative decisions mean, which can affect or even **negate** the influence of those decisions.

The judicial branch's powers aren't always clearly stated in the Constitution. Judicial powers have become more defined over the years. Congress has the power to establish and influence how the judicial system operates. For example, the Constitution doesn't say how many justices should be on the Supreme Court. That number is set by Congress and has changed several times over the years.

In 1954, after reviewing the *Brown v. Board of Education* case, the Supreme Court ruled that segregation in public schools was against the 14th Amendment and therefore unconstitutional. The lawyers who argued against segregation are seen here. From left to right are George E. C. Hayes, Thurgood Marshall, and James Nabrit.

The judicial branch has the power to review laws passed by Congress to determine if they're constitutional. Judicial review is not listed in the Constitution. Instead, the Supreme Court assumed this power after its ruling in the 1803 case *Marbury v. Madison*. This case came about because the newly elected president, Thomas Jefferson, rejected judges hired by the previous president, John Quincy Adams. Since then, judicial review has remained the judicial branch's most powerful check against the other branches.

The power of the judicial system can be seen in some of the amendments to the Constitution. The Fourth Amendment to the Constitution makes it illegal to search or seize a person's property without a warrant of the court. This is designed to limit the executive branch's power and ensure that all investigations are conducted reasonably and in accordance with the law.

JOHN MARSHALL

In the case of *Marbury v. Madison*, Chief Justice John Marshall said that it's the "duty of the Judicial Department to say what the law is." When laws conflict or appear in opposition to the Constitution, it's up to the Supreme Court to decide which law should apply to a case.

CHAPTER NINE

SEPARATION OF POWERS IN FRANCE

The democracy created by the Founding Fathers was admired and copied around the world. Shortly after the American Revolution, the people of France revolted against the French monarchy and the **feudal** system that had governed them for hundreds of years. The French Revolution was a long, bloody war, and it didn't solve all the country's problems. However, it helped change French politics.

Today, France's government is different from the U.S. government in several key ways. France's government has three branches, but the executive branch has two leaders. The president is directly elected by the people. The prime minister is appointed by the president and answers directly to Parliament, which is the bicameral legislative branch. The French legal system is divided into two parts: an administration branch and a judicial branch. A system of checks and balances exists between the branches and officials to help preserve justice and equality for the people of France.

In 1789, French revolutionaries stormed the Bastille, a fortress that symbolized the tyranny of the French monarchy. This event marked the beginning of the French Revolution, which lasted from 1789 until the late 1790s.

CHAPTER TEN

GOVERNMENTS OF THE WORLD

Today, many countries around the world have two-part and three-part governments with systems of checks and balances. These countries include Canada, Mexico, the United Kingdom, and others. These governments have key differences from the U.S. government, but they all include a separation of powers to help ensure fairness and equality for their citizens.

U.S. citizens are very fortunate to have a government that watches over itself and protects our freedoms. The citizens of some countries don't have the benefit of checks and balances in their governments. Imagine what life would be like if the president had the power to make, interpret, and execute laws without other branches to keep him in check. How do you think life would be different for U.S. citizens?

GLOSSARY

arbitrary (AR-buh-trehr-ee) Existing or coming about seemingly at random or by chance.

aristocracy (ayr-ih-STAH-kruh-see) A government run by a small, privileged class of people.

conservative (kuhn-SER-vuh-tihv) Believing in the value of established and traditional practices in politics and society.

conviction (kuhn-VIHK-shun) The act or process of finding a person guilty of a crime, especially in a court of law.

corruption (kuh-RUP-shun) Dishonest or illegal behavior, especially by someone in a position of power.

democratic (deh-muh-KRAA-tik) Relating to a system of government that favors social equality; also, having to do with the principles of democracy, or a government elected by the people.

desegregation (de-seh-gruh-GAY-shun) The act of removing segregation, or the separation of races in areas of society such as schools and public places.

feudal (FYOO-duhl) Referring to a system of government in which lords control the land and tenants farm it for very little in return.

liberal (LIH-buh-ruhl) Believing in the value of social and political change in order to achieve progress.

negate (nuh-GAYT) To deny something; to make invalid.

oppression (uh-PREH-shun) Unjust or cruel exercise of authority or power.

subpoena (suh-PEE-nuh) An order in writing commanding a person named in it to appear in court or face a penalty.

tyrant (TY-runt) A ruler who exercises total power harshly or cruelly.

INDEX

PRIMARY SOURCE LIST

Page 8
Portrait of John Locke. Oil on canvas. Sir Godfrey Kneller. 1697. Now held at the State Hermitage Museum, Saint Petersburg, Russia.

Page 17
Portrait of George Washington. Oil on canvas. Gilbert Stuart. 1797. Now held at the Clark Art Institute, Williamstown, MA.

Page 29
La prise de la Bastille (The Storming of the Bastille). Watercolor painting. Jean-Pierre Houël. 1789. Now held at the Bibliothèque nationale de France, Paris, France.

WEBSITES

Due to the changing nature of Internet links, PowerKids Press has developed an online list of websites related to the subject of this book. This site is updated regularly. Please use this link to access the list: www.powerkidslinks.com/sociv/sop